SOWING SEEDS

SOWING SEEDS

❀ LIFE LESSONS FROM MY FATHER ❀

Maurice R. Smith

FULL-SERVICE   BOOK-MAKERS

ESTD.   1999

I dedicate this writing to my sister Gina. One day she encouraged me to record stories about our father. I initially thought, *I don't think I have enough material worth writing. Besides,* I thought, *these are my memories, and who else would be interested?* She persisted. Gina said as an only son, I spent more time with our father than the daughters. As a result, I must have memories of our father my sisters likely did not experience. I relented and agreed to write an outline to see what could become of this.

Soon I had ten stories. The rest is history.

CONTENTS

This collection of short essays is a tribute to my father, James Wellington Smith. I have undertaken this task for a few reasons. First, the Holy Scriptures instructs us to honor our mother and father. Ephesians 6:1–3 reads, "*Children, obey your parents in the Lord: for this is right. Honour thy father and mother; (which is the first commandment with promise;) That it may be well with thee, and thou mayest live long on the earth.*" Thus I honor my father by remembering the life lessons he taught me.

The second reason for this tribute to my father is to memorialize the impressions he made on me. From my earliest memories, my father was an example to me of a man's duty to family, community, and mankind. He demonstrated in deeds and instructions that I have a responsibility to live a life worthy of being a Smith. You see, my father believed that a family name is a precious possession to be nurtured and protected. He placed on me a heavy charge to safeguard the family name and grow it to mean something more meaningful for future generations.

Finally, I honor my father because I do not want his essence to be lost for future generations. I believe it is important that each generation comes to understand the gifts they have in their genetic makeup from their ancestors. The trials and successes, predispositions and traits, and gifts and impediments make us who we are. So much of who and what we are comes from a line of family members. They enrich us. They give our lives deeper meaning. They are a part of us.

It has been over a decade since my father went to be with the Lord. I think of him most days. I miss our conversations. These are my stories about the life lessons he taught me. These lessons guide me to this day.

JAMES "BUBBA" WELLINGTON SMITH

JUNE 4, 1932–JULY 21, 2007

James "Bubba" Wellington Smith, of Southport, North Carolina, was born to Romia Smith and Mattie Smith Hewitt. My father attended Brunswick County Training School and served in the U.S. Air Force. My father excelled in various occupations, including longshoreman for the International Longshoremen's Association, real estate broker, farmer, deacon, Sunday school teacher, county commissioner, commissioner for the Employment Security Commission of North Carolina, and chairman of the Southeast Brunswick Sanitary District.

At the point of his passing, my father had been married to our mother, Rebecca Smith, for fifty-one years. Their children are Maurice R. Smith (spouse Diane) of Cary, North Carolina; Sharon C. Smith of Cary; Julie P. Webb (spouse Fred) of Sanford, North Carolina and Gina R. Smith of Clayton, North Carolina. Grandchildren are Rebecca C. Smith of Wake Forest, North Carolina; Maurice R. Smith II of Cary; Raven C. McQueen (spouse Cozell) of Durham, North Carolina, Fred D. Webb III of Raleigh, North Carolina, James K. Webb of Sanford; and Gabrielle P. Webb of Sanford.

My father was an extraordinary person in many respects. He was accomplished in business, public policy-making, community service and civic activities. My father was a thirty-second-degree Freemason. He held an authoritative perspective on the history and culture of Brunswick County and North Carolina. He showed a particular interest in Civil War artifacts, colonial living, and the American Revolution. He was a lifetime member of the Southport Historical Society. He understood the implications of history and sought to learn lessons that could be applied to future advancement.

My father loved the Lord and followed the principles of Jesus Christ in every area of his life. He believed deeply in the responsibility of charity. He was an angel to many who witnessed his benevolence. He felt a sense of duty to lend a helping hand to those less fortunate. My father sought no recognition or accolades for his charitable efforts. He simply and quietly went about his way of feeding the widows and orphans with a Christ-like spirit of love.

SETTING GOALS

One of the earliest lessons I learned from my father was the value of setting goals for my life. I chose this story to be the first of the short essays because it exemplifies the forethought my father placed in nearly every exchange we would share afterward. He would take ordinary everyday moments as an opportunity to teach me about life. More importantly, he would use these moments to illustrate how to be successful in life. Without saying so, I believe he felt that success came to those who lived a life of purpose. So seemingly it was his intention to instill in me a sense of purpose and direction for my life.

Living on a farm, there was always something to do ... something to learn. So it was on this day. I was twelve years old. I was working beside my father in the lower field of the farm, planting potatoes. He looked up from the hole he had just made in the ground with his hoe and suddenly asked me what I intended to do with the rest of my life. I thought for a moment and replied, "I don't know."

Even at the age of twelve I somehow knew this moment was going to be something extraordinary in my life. My father was a calculating thinker. He did not waste thoughts on mundane, pointless banter. He felt that every exchange needed to have a purpose. So I felt his question was meant to lead to something more profound.

My father explained that I did not have the luxury of going through life without direction. I must always be striving for something. He said it did not matter so much that I might change my mind later as to what my occupation would be. It was simply imperative that I always have a goal in front of me. So he expected me to choose now.

To some, part of my father's rationale may sound chauvinistic. He said to me that I had a heavy burden to be successful in life for the sake of a family I may someday have. Unlike my three younger sisters, it was inevitable that I would become the head of a household as an adult. With this position would come the responsibility to provide for my family. He said that my sisters may get married and be cared for by a husband. In my case, the role of providing sufficient means for my family would fall squarely to me.

My father said that if I did not choose a purpose for my life, he would assign a career choice for me. I remember pausing for what seemed like a long time. I wanted to be sure my first choice would be a good decision. Afraid to choose wrongly, I asked if I could have a day to think about it. He said, "Yes."

It is important to insert an observation about my father. He insisted there be a sense of purpose in everything he did. He also insisted I inherit this mandate for my life. He believed every task, journey, or endeavor should be pursued with expedience and urgency. He would often say that if I had nowhere to go, I should get there in a hurry. He did not like laziness. My father would always admonish me to go about life with determination.

The next day I accompanied my father on an errand to the bank. While standing in the lobby line of the Waccamaw Bank I noticed a man sitting in a corner office. He was wearing a crisp, white, long-sleeved shirt. He had papers on his desk. The large window allowed me to see the décor of his office, the certificates on his walls, and the nameplate on his desk. He looked important.

I turned and asked my father who that man was. My father replied, "That is the bank president." Without thinking further, I stated, "That is what I want to be: a bank president." What happened next illustrated my father's remarkable vision. His next statement would shape the rest of my life. Without hesitation, he answered, "Then you will need to go to college, major in business, and I will help you get there."

To put this lesson in perspective, we should consider the time and the place. This was 1969 in the South. The integration of our public schools had just taken place only a year before. I had never seen a black man in a white-collar position of authority. I had no role models after whom to pattern my ambitions. My father did not question my decision. He simply allowed me to dream.

During the ensuing years I would hold fast to my first choice to go into banking. My father would talk with me about the power of money and the importance of credit. He would highlight the disparities between the economic classes. He believed that poverty is linked to many societal ills. The gaps in education, healthcare, housing, and employment were exacerbated by the lack of economic power. I would come to adopt his doctrines and see myself as accepting a mission to help people with financial empowerment. The path for my future was set.

THE PRACTICAL APPLICATION

It is important to teach people to dream and have an ambition in life. The absence of a direction results in going through life aimlessly, taking whatever happenstance has to give. With goals, we have direction and a prescription for attaining our ambitions. This lesson is best instilled in young children, who are predisposed to imagining themselves as heroes, difference makers, and noble figures. Somewhere along the line, life happens, and we often lose our childlike enthusiasm for what could be.

Try this experiment. Ask small children what they would like to be when they grow up. Notice the responses you get. It is not so important what occupation, superhero role, or sport the children choose to excel in. I find the reaction most telling.

When children first begin to think about their future, they often go into a dreamlike state. They sit up straighter. They lift their heads. Their voices become a little more forceful. I believe this to be the case because children are looking forward and imagining a future full of possibilities. The operative words are "looking forward."

Planning for the future is a fundamental business practice. Words we use are budgeting, strategy, and projections. We readily accept the need to plot the future for our organizations but also accept the luck of the draw for our lives. My father knew better. He also believed that I needed to develop a discipline for lifelong goal setting at an early age.

There is an intrinsic value in thinking forward. Setting our minds on future endeavors disciplines us to put structure in our actions. Goals don't have to be detailed with particularity. The most important step in setting goals is establishing a direction.

The analogy I use here is making a journey. Let's say you plan to travel from North Carolina to New York but you have not yet decided the specific address. You have enough details to know that you are going to travel north. My father would say that you should get going. It is not necessary that you know the precise destination if you are committed to a direction. It is more important that you start. In some instances, the precise destination becomes clearer the closer one draws to a goal. If we never take the first and subsequent steps, we forsake the momentum necessary to accomplish the objective.

Goal setting has another positive benefit. When setting our minds toward a goal, we tend to lose sight of the present challenges. There will always be trials and tribulations in life. If we always look down at the shackles around our ankles, we will miss the opportunities on the horizons. Prudent people acknowledge the obstacles we face. An ambitious person constantly looks up and looks forward to new goals to accomplish.

Goals are hollow without actions. An ambition without a prospective motion is a wish. Wishes sometimes come true, but they are for dreamers only. I believe the drive to accomplish a goal greatly magnifies one's probability of success.

What's truly remarkable about this story is my father's reaction to a child's ambitions. My father had not been a banker. He had not attended college. On the surface, he was ill-equipped to help me achieve this goal. But I believed him. He believed in me. At the age of twelve, I was already a bank president in my and my father's mind.

BUYING PEACHES

t's 1992 and I have begun a new job. I am the executive vice president of the Local Government Federal Credit Union (LGFCU). I had resigned my position as the vice president of member education and training with the State Employees' Credit Union (SECU). My employment with SECU had begun in 1979.

Local Government Federal Credit Union is a financial cooperative that provides consumer services to local government employees, elected/appointed officials, volunteers, and their family members. In North Carolina, the ranks of local government include municipalities (cities, towns, villages), counties, fire departments, authorities (housing, airports), government councils, public-owned hospitals, parks and recreation, fire departments, and so on. Essentially, all political subdivisions below the state government level fall within the jurisdiction of local government.

I was the fifth employee on the LGFCU staff. Then the credit union's total assets were less than $70 million. In 1992, 33,680 members used the services of the credit union. Today, LGFCU employs over 180 employees, holds assets of more than $2 billion, and serves over 325,000 members. LGFCU is the fourteenth-largest depository financial institution in North Carolina. One in every thirty-three North Carolina citizens is a member of LGFCU.

As the executive vice president, my job duties were vast. I was assigned the responsibilities for marketing, policy development, credit oversight, and investments. Previously I had experience in all of these areas except investments. I found myself having to execute the purchase and sale of corporate investments. This would require developing new skills. I was sure I would learn the ropes.

Initially, my chief objective was to diversify the investment holdings and build a portfolio of marketable government-backed securities. The securities had to comply with all federal regulations for such instruments. I spent many hours and days consulting with Wall Street investment brokers and analysts. I had a steep learning curve to build my competencies in these activities.

I was particularly cautious in how these corporate investments would be made. It was clear from the beginning that there was risk with making investments with some brokers. There were chances that the persons with whom I was dealing were dishonest or incompetent. In either instance, my credit union could face losses if I made the wrong decision.

To manage a portfolio of marketable securities, I had to understand the fundamentals of pricing such instruments. One must consider the price, nominal rate, and duration of the instrument. The value of investments on our books can swing up or down depending on market conditions. Essentially, this is the effect of supply and demand on our portfolio.

For some reason, I had a mental block on under-standing the workings of these investments. I could eventually arrive at the right calculations. It just did not seem intuitive to me. I had to think carefully about each element of a transaction. I would often second-guess myself. I was not completely comfortable. I was embar-rassed to admit the insecurity. After all, I had taken eco-nomics in college. This should have been easier for me to understand. This indecision persisted for months.

One weekend I was visiting my parents in South-port, North Carolina. As I would often do during these visits, I shadowed my father around the farm attending to various chores. While in the fields on this day, my father asked me how I was doing on my new job. "Fine," I replied.

I thought for a moment more and decided to explain to him how marketable securities work. Having no financial institution experience, he might not fully understand these investments, or so I thought. At least the exercise would give me an opportunity to rehearse in my mind the steps to investment management.

I explained slowly how marketable securities work. I

told my father that the yields on these investments are determined by a stated rate and the price. I elaborated if the price is above par, then the yield is reduced because the rate remained steady. I ran through the process of seeking quotes from brokers, comparing fees, and executing the trade. I noted that these details require good timing, market information, and having the right relationships with the right firms.

After explaining the dynamics of investing, my father was silent. I thought perhaps he was confused. Maybe I did not explain the investments adequately. I was beginning to think this conversation was a mistake ... a waste of his time. After a few minutes, my father looked up briefly and said, "You are just buying and selling peaches." *What?* I thought. We were not talking about farm commodities at all. He must have not been listening to me. I started doubting myself again.

My father stopped what he was doing and explained himself. He asked, "Do you remember going with me to the farmers' market in Columbia, South Carolina, to buy produce?" "I do," I answered. He continued, "Do you remember that sometimes I would comment about the weather on the drive there? I nodded. He went on further on how he would mention to me how many trucks were in the peach orchards along the way. I said, "I thought we were just having small talk." He said no. He was commenting on the conditions we would face later that day at the market.

He reminded me that sometimes he purchased our peach stock as soon as we arrived. Other times he would wait for hours to purchase the inventory we needed. My father stated he was assessing market conditions and how might these factors affect the prices of peaches that day. Some days he would purchase an entire tractor-trailer truckload of peaches, far more than we needed. Later, we would unload what we needed and sell the balance of the load to other wholesale buyers at the farmers' market.

My father said peaches are like my marketable securities. The supply/demand on the farmers' market and the weather conditions affected the price we'd pay. The price influenced our profit margin or yield. He said, "When I bought an entire truckload, I was betting we could sell the excess inventory at a higher price than what we paid earlier. The absence of trucks in the fields and the forecast of thunderstorms indicated there would be a shortage of peach supplies that day. This often led to higher prices. This gave us the opportunity to buy low and sell high and make a quick profit off the margin."

My father asked if I noticed that he tended to buy his peaches from the same farmers week after week. I said I thought he was just being friendly. He said that was partly true. He went on to explain that it is important to know the quality and integrity of people with whom you do business. Your reputation to your customers may depend on your suppliers.

In the produce business, trust is important. An untrustworthy farmer might pack the bottom of his bushel baskets with low-grade peaches and put the premium peaches on top. My father said that when he is buying one hundred baskets of peaches, there's no time to inspect each basket. One must trust that the farmer's goods are what he represents on the surface.

My father said, "Peach farmers are like security brokers. They can only sell you what they have. The prices can change. Trust is essential because the investments may not be the value you thought you were getting."

My father paused. "You see, Son, you are just buying and selling peaches." I never misunderstood marketable securities again.

-《《◆》》-

THE PRACTICAL APPLICATION

To be successful in life, one should take advantage of every resource available. One of the most important tools we have is our experience. Experiences shape who we are, our character, and our perspective on life. It is imperative that we realize that each experience serves a useful purpose.

The lesson I learned here was to not discount any experiences. During all those trips to the farmers' market, I missed the subtle life lessons my father was showing me. I failed to recognize that even the most ordinary of moments can be a teaching experience.

This episode with my father opened my eyes to explore my past more closely. I wonder to this day what other experiences I had that would have been relevant to past trials and opportunities. Whenever I encounter a challenge or new prospect, I reflect on my experiences—what have I seen, heard, or felt that can provide guidance for the situation at hand.

I learned that experiences must be mined like precious materials. If one only scratches the surface, important discoveries could remain uncovered. If one digs indiscriminately, important revelations, like fine jewels, can be overlooked. Some experiences are hidden in our minds just waiting to be rediscovered. It is up to us to be alert to the lessons that remain to be told and retold.

It is a tricky proposition to mine for experiences that may seem relevant to new situations. Exploring experiences requires one to look for interactions that may seem unrelated to the current fact patterns. The obvious subject matter of an experience may seem remote to the challenges of the day. At first I did not see the link between peaches and marketable securities. I found it particularly striking that my father was preparing me for a position in financial services twenty-five years before I would need the skills.

I believe experiences are our secret weapons in life. My experiences are mine. They have uniquely shaped me. Even if I witness an event at the same time as others,

I have a singular perspective, because I make sense of the event through the backdrop of my experiences. This makes my perspective different.

I have learned to filter new moments through the lens of my experiences. Because of my background and life journey, I am supposed to see the world differently. This is not necessarily a case of right and wrong. This is just my system for making sense of what confronts me. I can't turn off my experiences. I should, however, embrace and exploit them for my advantage.

I have learned to appreciate the experiences we carry. Our experiences give us an edge and angle no one can predict or copy. If you want a more successful future, find new meanings in your experiences. You have new lessons to learn by revisiting your past.

UNTANGLING PROBLEMS

My hometown, Southport, North Carolina, is a port city that sits at the mouth of the Cape Fear River as it spills into the Atlantic Ocean. Southport is known for its nearby beaches, seafood industry, and marine tourism. It is a favorite destination for vacation goers, boaters, and fishermen seeking to be near the water.

You would think growing up in a small seaside town would instill in me a predisposition to water activities. The opposite is the fact. I'm not a good swimmer. As a child I preferred to spend my recreational time in the woods, hunting, hiking, and camping. Staying on dry land suited me just fine.

Even to a landlubber, the beauty and the lure of the ocean were undeniable. I could sit on the dock and watch the waves for hours. To me, the water is a beautiful backdrop.

I suspect my father thought of the ocean differently. To him, the sea was a big field ready to be harvested. You see, my father's father was a commercial fisherman. My father learned to fish and navigate the waters from my grandfather. To say that my father was an accomplished boatman is to put it mildly. Somehow, I did not inherit that gene.

One day, Father decided to take me fishing off one of the downtown piers. We were using rods and reels that took an exacting skill. One had to know how much slack to have in the line, how to cast, and the proper technique to haul in a catch. I struggled to learn the nuances of fishing.

At one point, my reel became tangled with the fishing line. I pulled and pulled tighter to squeeze the line back onto the spindle. The line became clustered and eventually jammed the whole mechanism. I looked up and noticed that my father must have been watching me the whole time. I thought he might be angry that I fouled up his fishing gear. I asked for help, and he walked over toward me.

He asked, "What's the problem?" I said the fishing line is tangled around the reel. He questioned further. "Where does the problem begin?" he inquired. I said, "I don't know. It's just one big ball of mangled fishing line." He chuckled.

My father took the fishing pole from me and proceeded to teach me a life lesson. He tugged on the edges of the tangled fishing line until the bale was several times larger. The fishing lines were no longer tightly packed together. I could see between the lines. He reached into the now loose ball of fishing line and methodically retreaded the spindle until all the line was neatly back in place. I asked how he did that. My father said, "Son, fishing is like life. To clear up a mess, sometimes you have to make a bigger mess."

My father said it's hard to fix a problem when it looks like one big, tangled mess. He instructed me to find the simplicity in complex challenges. He noted that most solutions come from simple applications. We make them complicated because we think the answer must match the intensity of the problem.

Afterward, my father handed the rod and reel back to me. He did not admonish me to avoid making another mess. He simply said, "If this happens again, you now know how to bail yourself out."

THE PRACTICAL APPLICATION

I don't want to sound pessimistic. Life has its challenges. The outcome of these problems often depends on our approach to the situation at hand.

The thing about problems is that the underlying factors often are masked in the noise of circumstances. We often attempt to tackle the big issue without having a full appreciation for the factors that led to the problems. A singular problem on its face may be a series of smaller challenges that are lurking beneath the surface. When one attempts to resolve an apparent problem without addressing the contributing elements, there is a risk that the problem will be made worse.

For instance, you have been made aware of a problem

in your business or your family. Your first instinct may be to jump in and fix the problem. But you must ask yourself what the real problem is. What you have seen so far may just be the symptoms of a problem. Attacking the symptoms may still leave the problem to fester further.

Discovering the authentic problem may mean that one must make a bigger mess. People get uncomfortable when leaders ask questions and begin an inquisition. To solve a problem, you may need to challenge all assumptions. To do so requires some digging. You should question sources and test presumptions. You should be prepared to face the truth no matter where it leads you.

Admittedly, I have a propensity to solve problems quickly. This is a good trait when the proverbial barn is on fire. Some problems require an immediate and decisive solution. In these instances, fast, definitive action is necessary. Not all problems start with instantaneous combustion. Some problems fester for a long time before igniting into a full-blown disaster.

I learned from my father the importance of analyzing a problem for its contributing factors. If some elements remain unaddressed, the risk of an incomplete resolution remains. I used this perspective to assist me in the art of alternative dispute resolution.

I became a Certified Superior Court Mediator because I wanted to learn the skills of advanced problem solving. Certified mediators are trained to help clients work through complex disagreements and arrive at a mutually acceptable remedy. In many instances, the solution to a dispute is not immediately apparent to either side. The certified mediator has to be skilled at the craft of reading between the lines of communications. The parties often need to be coached to recognize a workable alternative to litigation. This usually involves exploring what each side recognizes as the real friction points.

Whether in litigation, business disputes, or family squabbles, the art of problem solving is a vital skill. Solving challenges requires the ability to untangle problems. My father understood this important fact. This lesson would benefit me in multiple ways for years to come.

A clear example of a lesson I learned about problem-solving came in law school in a trial practice exercise. The professor was trying to instill in the students the need to be alert to the clues a client gives in how to solve their problems.

In this instance, we were assigned to interview volunteers from the community who were posing as clients. The volunteer clients were given a hypothetical problem with an underlying legal issue embedded in the story. Our task was to interview our respective clients and tease out the issues, apply the law, and recommend a course of action.

I met my client and began the conversation by asking a series of probing, open-ended questions. I noticed the client was fairly reserved. She was not particularly accommodating. I had to persist to get to what I thought was the issue. I thought I retrieved all I needed to know and made a decision on what legal remedies were justified. I later learned I missed some key indicators of what the client was actually seeking.

The professor criticized my work product. He noted I was too quick to focus on the seemingly obvious problem. He suggested that I relax and let the facts come to me. He said, given enough time and patience, most situations reveal themselves fully.

A CHOCOLATE MILKSHAKE

G rowing up in a small town offered limited options for fast-food dining. It was a big deal when a Hardee's hamburger franchise opened in town. Until then, the few options included a handful of homegrown restaurants. One of my favorite fast-food joints was the Little Mint.

The Little Mint offered an array of food selections. Hamburgers, pizza, and fried chicken were the main staples on the menu. My favorite choice was the quarter dark chicken meal. This item featured two pieces of dark meat chicken, a serving of coleslaw, a roll, and french-fried potatoes. The Little Mint also offered a variety of drinks, including milkshakes.

One summer afternoon my father and I were sitting at a picnic table under one of the pecan trees on the family farm. This was unusual for us because it seems we were always doing something or attending to farm chores. My father turned to me and asked me to go to the Little Mint to buy him a chocolate milkshake. After he handed me some money I was on my way.

I arrived and placed the order. I was surprised to learn that the Little Mint did not offer chocolate milkshakes. They had vanilla and strawberry shakes. I returned home empty-handed.

Upon returning home, my father asked where his milkshake was. I told him that the Little Mint did not sell chocolate milkshakes. He smiled for a moment and said he knew that. This was the exact moment I realized this was no ordinary errand.

My father proceeded to cross-examine me. He questioned why I decided to return home empty-handed. I said, "Your instructions were to purchase a chocolate milkshake from the Little Mint. Since the Little Mint does not offer chocolate milkshakes, I figured the task was impossible." There was nothing more to do except return home.

He asked, "Why didn't you substitute the flavor for another kind of milkshake? Did you think the flavor was the most important part of the instructions?" he continued. I thought for a moment. I replied, "You specifically asked for chocolate, so the flavor must have been an important ingredient."

He persisted, "You could have gone to Hardee's and purchased a chocolate milkshake. Did you believe that the Little Mint was your only choice of restaurants?" He said, "You were presented with a problem. The place where I requested a milkshake was unable to fulfill my request. You had options, yet you chose to return home without any milkshakes. Why?"

I thought for a moment. I thought he was looking for a reason for my failure. I said, "I have no excuses." I felt bad because I did not want to disappoint the person I idolized the most in my life. I did not know how to fix this.

My father said, "Sit down, Son." He explained that he was not looking for excuses. He sent me on this errand to teach me a lesson. He wanted to understand my thought processes in making decisions when confronted with an impossible task. My father went on with his explanation.

He stated, "In life you must make decisions in all manner of situations. In many cases, the conclusion you arrive at isn't what's important. What's important is your ability to use reasoning to decide." He said most decisions are made with imperfect information. Along the way, we learn that we don't have all the facts. "The problem occurs when we believe we know everything. This is when we neglect to look for new solutions. You had multiple ways to fix the problem you were presented. You made one of many decisions that could have been taken. I wanted to know how you reached your conclusion."

My father said one day I would grow up and become a businessman. He said, "Son, you will be expected to make important decisions that will affect your company, customers, employees, and career. In some cases, the decisions you make will determine the ultimate success or failure of the organization. You need to know the discipline of decision-making."

My father explained that it is crucial to make deliberate decisions. More importantly, he said I should be able to defend the rationale for my decisions. It is inexcusable to reply to a call to justify a decision with a shrug of a shoulder and say, "I don't know." This would suggest an illogical course of action that he would find unacceptable for a businessman.

I asked my father what would have been the right decision. Should I have bought a chocolate milkshake from somewhere else? Should I have substituted another flavor of milkshake for the chocolate? He reemphasized this was never about the chocolate milkshake. He said he was not particularly thirsty. He wanted to see what my reaction would be and how I would go about arriving at my decision.

I neglected to push my father more on what would he have done. I still wonder to this day.

THE PRACTICAL APPLICATION

The chocolate milkshake dilemma is about decision-making. I have learned in life how important it is to make good decisions. The most valuable decision-making skill is the ability to find an opportunity in a seemingly impossible task. This requires keen executive wherewithal and knowing how to prioritize the information you are given.

Throughout my career, with my family and community activities, I have had to make decisions. In retrospect, some choices were good selections. Other decisions were misguided. Some decisions were good but had unfortunate results. Just because a decision is the right option does not mean all will end well. Good decisions just mean you were justified in making that choice. The outcomes of our decisions are sometimes determined by factors outside our control or vision.

I have not made any decisions with the intention of seeking a bad result. In each instance, I thought I knew enough and was prepared to handle the consequences. Clearly, I was not always right. So, what are the key elements for making good decisions? Let's apply the lessons learned from the chocolate milkshake dilemma.

First, be sure to understand the demands placed upon you. My father gave me incomplete instructions. I would later realize that this was intentional. I could have taken one of various courses of action. I chose an action without fully considering the other choices. I failed to fully understand my options.

This is the case with choices we all make in life. In

some situations, our decisions might have been different if were privy to alternative options. We may have invested differently. We could have applied our talents to another industry. We might have applied ourselves more diligently in school. We might have different social circles. Having more than one option does not mean we will make good decisions. The multitude of possible paths just means we will have the opportunity to reassess our decision before we fully commit to a direction.

A practical lesson to be taken from the chocolate milkshake challenge is to avoid seeing problems as binary choices. My observation is that most issues do not present either/or alternatives exclusively. Options are neither black nor white, conservative or liberal, or up or down. If we limit our choices to a few obvious selections, we risk missing creative solutions that could be more effective.

Throughout my career I have witnessed businesses and individuals make bad choices. There are lots of reasons for strategic errors. In most instances we can summarize the cause as a lack of awareness for creative options. In other words, the decision-maker fell for the quick-draw solutions of a binary set of choices.

In hindsight, we can often revisit a decision and reach an understanding of where we went wrong. As refreshing as this enlightenment may be, it is often too late to change the outcome of the fact pattern in play. Perhaps we learn a good lesson for the next time we encounter a similar scenario.

I believe the most effective antidote for binary-choice thinking is to back up and take a broader perspective. A professor from Stanford University offered me an approach for solving complex problems. He said to literally get up from my desk, leave the office, and return as if I were my successor. My eyes should be wide open to the possibilities. I would not be beholden to past decisions. I should be divorced from the emotional ties to previous courses of action. I should ask a few critical questions:

- What result do I ultimately desire here?
- What has led to the obstacles I face?
- What is the origin of this challenge?
- What would a detached, new actor do in my situation?

These questions are not magical or prescriptive. One can substitute a bank of wholly different inquiries. The important aspect of this exercise is to consider new choices from a wider point of view. Then one is able to escape the binary-choice trap.

Second, we should understand the priorities placed upon us. My father was specific. He asked for a chocolate milkshake from the Little Mint. In this request, there were several conditions to his request. He specified the beverage he wanted: *a milkshake*. He indicated the flavor: *chocolate*. The directive included a particular restaurant: *the Little Mint*. Had I been adept at the art of decision-making, I would have chosen to assign a level of priority on the conditions. Was it more important that the milkshake be chocolate or come from the Little Mint, or could a chocolate drink have been sufficient?

Decisions often entail multiple demands. With each settlement on a demand, we risk forsaking other choices. In economics, this is called the opportunity cost. Any choice we make is weighed against the next best choice that is available to us. It is important to know that every decision comes with a choice, opportunity, or consequence. If we fully consider that our decisions have costs associated with them, then it may be prudent to understand the price.

When making decisions, I have found it useful to establish a ranking of the most important to least important choices that are before me. If I'm going to forgo a choice, I prefer the difference to be on a matter that is not as important as the choice I've made. This exercise offers us the opportunity to prioritize our choices into a rank order. With this ranking in place, I seek to fulfill the most important demands first, then the second most important demand, and so forth.

Third, we should be prepared to defend our position. I was not ready for the chocolate milkshake test. While my father did not give me a grade, I felt that I failed. I made my decision without grasping my options or understanding that I had options in the first place. To make matters worse, I did not adequately defend my position.

My father was preparing me for leadership. This leadership would extend to the community, my job, and my family. Leadership by its very definition implies there will be followers. Leadership carries with it a burden to defend oneself to one's followers. While followers look to the leader for direction, they will not easily surrender their right to cast judgment on the leader's effectiveness. The act of defending one's position is a moment for the leader to affirm his convictions, decisions, and assumptions. If the leader is unable to defend a decision, the decision should rightfully be challenged.

A good decision can be defended. A bad decision can be defended as well. In fact, through the art of persuasion, a bad decision can appear good. The most important consideration here is the analytical exercise of mounting a defense. When a leader feels she does not have to defend a decision, the risk of failure is exaggerated by hubris.

The act of considering a decision defense is a good test of one's decision. I mentioned earlier that most decisions are made with imprecise information. What we lack in facts is often substituted with assumptions, beliefs, biases, and guesses. These gap-fillers should be vetted to ensure that the decision is as practical as it should be. To prove the gap-fillers, we should invite challenges. The defense to the challenges fortifies our decision or disproves our position before we make a commitment.

Here's my final observation on decision-making. A decision is made at a point in time with fixed information. As soon as the decision is reached, the landscape changes. Second-guessing one's decisions is useful for assessing our analytical abilities and performance. We should keep in mind that only hindsight yields a clear perspective.

LEARN FROM OTHERS' EXPERIENCES

My father was a student of history. He was absolutely enthralled with the tales of a time long ago. He collected Civil War artifacts. He visited wooded sites of colonial settlements with a metal detector in search of historical relics. My father would visit the state library in Raleigh, North Carolina, to get copies of eighteenth-century maps to learn about the locations of old roads, homesteads, and trading routes. He was a member of the Southport Historical Society and supported its mission to preserve and discover history. My father did not do anything without a reason. It would seem his interest in history was for the purpose of gaining insight for the future.

This insight would be used to predict future behavior that would benefit him.

My father told me once that one of his most important responsibilities was to help me avoid mistakes. By his own account, he admitted to making mistakes in life. He said his role was to point out pitfalls in life that I would certainly come across and advise me to stay clear of them. He used the metaphor of a road to illustrate the point.

He stated that if he identified a pothole in the road and I proceeded to drive into it, then it was my fault for ignoring his advice and not heeding the warning. If he knows of a hazard in my way and he fails to point out the pothole and I drive into it, then that's on him. He would often tell me that he has a PhD in living and I could benefit from his experience. I have indeed. Here are two illustrations where my father used the experiences of others to help direct my path.

First, my father was an incessant newspaper reader. He read the newspaper every day from cover to cover. He was fascinated with the stories of others' lives and the tales of events in our community and world. He was particularly focused on articles about business and commerce. I thought he was just seeking to be informed on the day's events. That was part of the reason for surveying the newspaper. There was another reason.

One day, my father advised me to read the newspaper daily. He said that, when I do, I shouldn't just read the good news stories. In fact, I should focus on the bad news. In particular, I should study with great interest the stories about scandals, business failures, and disgraced officials. I asked why. He stated that these stories are potential potholes in the road, and I should make note of what to avoid.

He explained. "For instance, when the newspaper covers a story about a celebrity or public figure who has made a colossal mistake, pay close attention to the underlying assertions." He said don't be distracted by the salacious facts. Underlying the hype is a story of choices someone made that led them to a problem. If I understand how this person's life went awry, then I have the makings of a warning of what not to do. In other words, the person in the newspaper pointed out a pothole to me, and I should take the warning to avoid making the same mistake.

Newspaper scandals are useful for illustrating how to react when something has gone bad. Some people choose to lash out against their political adversaries. Others run and hide from the public. Some people make matters worse by exacerbating the situation with more bad conduct. My father stated that I should learn what approaches work for which situations. When the inevitable troubles come my way, I should have a recipe for what to do that will serve me best.

My father also elaborated on the nature of problems in which one finds oneself. When we read in the newspaper about a controversy, the matter has boiled to the point that it is now a public-interest story. This is not usually when the problem began. Long before the newspaper decided to cover the story, a series of decisions had likely led to this bad outcome. One should seek to understand how another's path to a catastrophe started, so as to avoid the trend altogether.

My father used climbing out on a tree branch as a metaphor for this lesson. Consider a situation where someone is out on a tree branch at the point it may break. That is a problem. But the problem did not begin at that moment. The decision to climb out from a limb onto a branch preceded the problem. The decision to leave the trunk of the tree and move onto the limb occurred earlier. The decision to bark up the wrong tree may be the initiating event that started the ultimate calamity.

My father insisted that most bad decisions did not start with the headline news. A series of bad decisions led to the calamitous results. If we trace the steps back to the beginning, we may see that the first bad choice might have seemed innocent on its face. That bad decision led to another bad decision that may have been marginally worse but, taken alone, did not seem prohibitive. The series of decisions were likely weighed on a per-transaction basis. The actor did not consider just how far the series of bad decisions had taken him from the base position. Soon, he would find himself out on a limb with little support. My father advised that I must always keep a grounded eye on the right path; otherwise I might find myself astray from my course.

Second, my father used my experiences in finance as a path for learning further. He instructed me to see this position as more than a mere job.

My first job after graduation from undergraduate school in 1979 was as a loan officer for the State Employees' Credit Union. The position description included such responsibilities as receiving applications for credit, assisting the office with administrative tasks, collecting delinquent accounts, opening new accounts, and providing financial counseling to members. I received members in my office, listened to their stories, and applied our credit standards to the facts that were presented to see if the loan application may be approved.

My father was always interested in my career. Every job I had attracted his attention. He would ask questions about what I had learned, what training I had undergone, and how I went about the duties I assumed. Of all the positions I had occupied, the loan officer position seemed to capture his attention the most.

As a loan officer, my father told me, I had a front-row seat to many of life's lessons. This was an opportunity to learn from others' experiences. Unlike most people who only learn from first-account lessons, I had the opportunity to learn from members who freely told me their stories.

Applicants who request a loan often need to provide a candid picture of their financial situation. In some instances, members need money because they are in financial distress. In other cases, loan requests are for farsighted purposes. In all situations, members shared their stories.

My father said the stories I heard from loan applicants represented two opportunities. Some stories illustrated warnings of what mistakes to avoid. These stories involved tales of bad judgments about financial decisions. Some stories highlighted positive examples of behavior I should emulate. Every story offered lessons worthy of heeding.

My father used these examples to ensure that I recognized the opportunity for learning lessons from others' experiences. I am grateful for his advice and counsel. I have used his encouragement to learn from the experiences of people all around me.

-‹‹‹◆›››-

THE PRACTICAL APPLICATION

When people make colossal mistakes, we can usually trace the blunder back to a series of decisions. With each decision, the decision-maker believed the act was a prudent choice or of little consequence. This is premised on the assumption that most people don't set out to make bad decisions from which there is no easy recovery. These sequential acts of bad decisions seem innocent and insignificant individually. Taken as a whole, the result is an outcome that can be disastrous.

Organizations are in the business of taking risks for the benefit of their stakeholders. Such risks include speculation with new products, emerging markets, and financial gambles. When considering taking a risk, an executive may engage in a type of modeling to make the best decision.

Modeling takes a set of circumstances and applies the facts to a proven rule or process. Facts are usually disorderly; they come in an irrational order and often contain the noise of irrelevant information. Modeling rules help organize facts into a rational order. When subject to industry, regulatory, legal, or procedural rules, decision-making becomes more manageable when a modeling template is applied to the information.

Modeling often involves a review of case studies,

which are examinations of others' experiences with similar circumstances and predicaments. One can learn a great deal from others who have faced a comparable question. The benefit comes from learning what worked and may be emulated. Also, case studies uncover warnings for what efforts fell short of expectations. To get a balanced viewpoint, one should look at both perspectives.

Another important feature of modeling is the practice of making projections. When facing a decision that has consequences down the road, it is vital to consider the probable outcomes. Projections map the likely results of a course of action when applied to the various paths to an objective.

It may be helpful to imagine the natural course of a decision and the downstream effect of the choices. Imagine that you are faced with a choice of options. Think of your choices like you would sketch a flowchart. Now, choose one option and think about the logical outcome of that choice. How might others react to your choice? What are the costs of that choice? What opportunities are you forgoing for the choice? Undertake the same exercise for the next decision node in the flowchart. If this path of decisions leads you to an unacceptable place, you have ample warning not to pursue that course.

Techniques such as modeling, case study reviews, and projections are routine business applications. Organizations employ these tools throughout various industries. These processes are not reserved for commercial entities only. One could use the same techniques for personal decisions. These tools are merely formalized versions of the lessons my father taught me.

When one has a consequential decision to make, a heightened level of scrutiny should be applied to the facts and options. A consequential decision is one that has important ramifications for one's life and career. This is the moment when a person can change the course of his vocation or alter the direction of her life. Given that these tools work for businesses, one should consider how personal benefits could be gained from following the same disciplines.

A LESSON FOR WORKING HARD

My father was a hard worker. Most of my memories of him are in settings where he was working diligently. It seems he worked seven days per week, from sunup into the late evening hours. His work ethic influenced me more than any other example he demonstrated.

My father's work experience included a variety of occupations. He worked as a shoeshine boy as a youngster. He was a deckhand on his father's shrimp boat operation. He was a radio operator in the U.S. Air Force. His civilian adult work experiences included roles as bartender, longshoreman, farmer, real estate broker, county commissioner, and governor appointee to a state agency. My father obviously had talents in multiple areas and did not hesitate to learn new skills.

I remember many days when my father would leave one job and immediately undertake another. It was not uncommon for him to return home from his longshoreman job, work on the farm for hours, and then drive to the farmers' market to procure wholesale inventory for our roadside produce market.

When I was too young to operate the farm tractor unsupervised, he would leave instructions for what I could do. Often my task was to have the tractor readied with the right equipment so that when he arrived from the docks at Sunny Point Military Base, he could immediately begin to till the fields.

The type of work in which my father was involved was tough and backbreaking. He would get sunburns in the hot summer days and frostbite from bitterly cold winter nights on the decks of container ships. My father seemed to have a dogged determination to succeed. Hard work was his approach to accomplish his goals.

Living on a farm, there was always more work to perform than hours in a day to complete the tasks. Every day, my father and I had an assignment for the season. We were always planting a crop, cultivating a crop, harvesting a crop, or getting ready to plant the next crop.

My father seemed to never weary of the hard work. Surely, the persistent daily grind of unceasing demands took a toll on him. But this is mere speculation, because he never complained to me or showed signs of fatigue.

I admit I would grow somewhat tired of always working. I spent most of my days on the farm. I had regular chores to perform. There was little time for recreation. I discovered as a teenager that my days were different from those of many of my friends.

At school, my friends would talk about hanging out on the street corners. They would laugh about the good times they had. They would share tales of funny antics and friendly pranks. I was convinced I was missing something great by always being on the farm away from the corner.

When I was a young teenager, I asked my father if I could join the fellas on the corner. He answered, "No." He just said, "No." No explanation or reason was given. I was a bit disappointed, but I respected my father too much to protest. I simply went back to work on the farm.

Every now and then, I would return to the notion that it would be more fun on the corner than in the fields. When I would run errands in town to the post office or the bank, I would see the guys sitting on the corner seemingly having so much fun. I would return to my father with a new appeal to go hang out on the corner. He would reply with the same answer: "No." After a while, I put the idea aside and only focused on my work obligations.

One day, around the age of seventeen, I became interested in the street corner again. I asked my father once more if I could hang out on the corner with the guys after I finished my chores. I did not expect a different result. Yet I asked again. This time he said, "Yes."

My father's answer shocked me. I did not know what to think about his sudden change of mind. Nevertheless, I hurriedly finished my jobs, rushed to wash away the field dirt, and put on a clean change of clothes. I hopped in our 1969 Corvair and drove to the spot where I was sure I would find the boys on the corner.

Just as I expected, I found the fellas on the same corner adjacent to the middle school. I spoke to the gang. They greeted me with friendly gestures. I took a seat on the curb among them and eagerly anticipated the freedom I would finally enjoy.

What happened next surprised me. After a short period of time, I began feeling restless. The conversation felt trivial. Much of the time was spent watching cars pass by. Every so often, there was a debate about sports, girls, or some current event.

I turned to my cousin and asked what happens next. He said, "Nothing much." I wanted to know what we'd be doing later in the day. He said this is pretty much what they do every day. I waited for another half hour and saw no movement. I told the guys I would see them later. I returned home.

When I arrived back on the farm, my father did not seem surprised to see me so soon. He asked if I enjoyed my time with the guys on the corner. I told him they were not doing anything. They are just sitting on the corner wasting time. My father said nothing. He smiled at me and went back to work. I never returned to the corner.

-≺≺≺◆≫≫-

THE PRACTICAL APPLICATION

When I entered the business world my father told me chances are I would not always be the smartest or most talented person in the room. He said, "Some may have more experience than you. Some will have political connections that could dwarf your networks. Some will come from families that have exposed them to cultural insights that could make them seem worldlier."

My father said that, in the presence of people who appear more qualified than I was, I may be inclined to feel less adequate. He said, "Don't! You have an advantage that evens the playing field. You were raised on a farm to know the value of work. Others might be smarter, but no one should be able to outwork you." I have taken this advice to be my competitive advantage.

I have observed that people generally have two kinds of advantages available to them in life. One type of edge comes from a natural-born talent—the instinctive aptitude some people have for athletics, music, entertainment, science, and other endeavors. Their skills come easily without much struggle. These folks have abilities that elude many people.

The other advantage comes from persistent hard work. These folks hone their skills through an extraordinary work ethic. They outwork others to gain a competitive edge over their rivals. Individuals who know how to work feverishly can often achieve positive results because they apply tenacious attention to reaching their goals.

The world of business is not sympathetic. Organizations seek a competitive advantage against rivals. Such is often the case with employees within each company as well. Students in a classroom can act the same way. Competition exists at nearly every level of society. One could become complacent and settle for being a run-of-the-mill person, or one could strive to surpass expectations by performing at the highest level he can muster. Because many people don't know how to work—I mean *really* work—there is an opportunity to get ahead of the crowd.

There are several examples in my life where I chose to apply the principle of hard work to attain a goal. In some instances, I wanted certain jobs because I believed the positions would lead to great opportunities. The application process called for an application and résumé to be submitted. I went beyond the minimum and prepared a business case for my hiring. Often I included a portfolio of past work products and analyses of the results. I imagined myself in the position and submitted what I had imagined would be the work plan for the next six months. I wanted the interviewer to see that I would be a hard worker if chosen. The preparation paid off. Afterward I would work feverishly to validate that I was the right choice.

When I went to law school at age forty-four I was a bit intimidated by the younger classmates who seemed to have been bred for the curriculum. Some came from a long line of lawyers in their family. Some worked in law offices as paralegals and understood the lingo. In a moment of uncertainty I expressed my doubt to my father. He reminded me from whence I had come. He said hard work would be my secret weapon. "Don't let anyone outwork you," he commanded.

In law school I felt compelled to work harder than ever. It was not enough to read the assigned text of the chapter and answer a few questions. I prepared outlines, made up acronyms as mnemonics, devised new study tips, read secondary materials, and built templates comparing various views. All this could have been excessive, but I did not know how to do anything but keep working. After one exam, the professor noticed my technique and commented that he had seen this approach before. I think he may have been hinting that it was overkill. No matter to me; this was my secret weapon.

Nothing is distinctively proprietary about the principle of hard work. The ability to work hard is available to anyone willing to be persistent. This trait requires determination and focus. A strong work ethic takes the willpower to plow through obstacles. The commitment to hard work also takes leadership. If a person finds herself in an environment where mediocrity is the norm, she must decide for herself that extraordinary results require extraordinary effort. Whether someone has natural-born talents or not, hard work improves the probability of success.

Some distractions to hard work can plague anyone. For people who lose focus and discipline, these detours could easily misguide them and influence them to get off track.

So often I have witnessed friends and colleagues pattern their behavior after unproductive examples. Seldom does this course of direction produce good results.

A few tell-tale signs identify a person as not being a hard worker. In some instances, if one settles for a standard that is less than the very best, this person is not a hard worker. I've often heard people say that a completed task is "good enough." "Good enough" implies room for improvement. If there is daylight between the performance submitted and any level of something better, the work was not its best. Performing less than the best is acceptable if that is the highest performance from that worker. Less than the best is not okay if the worker intentionally withdrew from the engagement prematurely.

An individual who patterns himself after the low performer in an organization is not a hard worker. It puzzles me that some individuals weigh their performance based on the work of other low performers. If a person compares his workmanship to individuals who knowingly work at a subpar level, this signals he is not a hard worker. In a way, the person who copies an obvious nonperformer is worse than the nonperformer. The nonperformer may actually be ignorant to his lack of production. The person who emulates the nonperformer intentionally decides to be a nonperformer, which spells a greater malfeasance.

Most people know who the nonperformers are in their organization. They consistently arrive late for work. They stay out longer on breaks. They hang out at the proverbial watercooler longer. They talk too much. They complain too much. They submit their work assignments after the deadlines. Shall I go on?

Hard workers find complacency agonizing. It runs against the grain of a hard worker to sit idly by and accept nonproductivity. Someone who accepts that a situation is as good as it gets is forfeiting the ambition to do anything about it. If she opts for inaction, she fails. My father would demand that I not tolerate nonperformance for myself and work to do something about it.

SEEK GOOD ADVICE

My father showed me several examples of the importance of seeking help when one needs guidance. He was not particularly impressed with individuals' educational credentials. My father valued the work experience of people who have proven themselves as evidenced by their body of work. He seemed to find more enjoyment in learning from people whom society discounted as being less important. These are the folks to whom he would pay the most attention.

My father and mother purchased a thirty-acre family vegetable farm when I was a young boy. My father had not worked on a farm before. He knew very little about farming. For some reason, he wanted to be a farmer. He knew he needed help learning the craft of farming. He sought counsel from other farmers who had already mastered the skills of agriculture.

In the early years on the farm my father learned from his mistakes. He learned the importance of crop rotation for preserving the nutrients in the soil. An old farmer showed him how to plant corn by leaving a path every four rows so that the tractor could navigate in the fields during harvest time. Each year my father would pick up new tips and tactics from area farmers on what crops to plant and how to cultivate the fields.

When we would travel to the farmers' market, my father would spend time talking with other farmers about the types of seeds they preferred. He would sit on the tailgates of their pickup trucks and ask for advice on how to increase yields, ward off pests, select the best fertilizers, and make the best of off-season preparations.

My father could have taken college classes to learn about farming. He told me that if one wants to do a job, ask people who have already proven themselves in the craft. His way of doing this was to speak to old farmers whose experiences produced a body of work that evidenced their competence.

My father taught me to look for advice in some unlikely places. He said that an empty wagon makes the most noise. His point was that not everyone who offers advice is a credible source. In some instances I should look beyond the obvious to find people who possess unique perspectives.

My father said that getting good advice requires a two-way exchange. One should first seek to gain a relationship with others who can help you, which means getting to know someone long before you might need them. When and if the time should arise when you need help, the adviser will be more inclined to give you advice.

The lessons I was taught on good advice included the teachings that relevant guidance depends greatly on facts and circumstances. When my father sought farming advice he approached farmers. When he needed financial guidance he talked with our family banker. My father said I should not ask a plumber about farming if he lacks the requisite skills in that area.

I asked my father who is at fault if I should heed bad

advice. He said the burden is on me to prove the reliability of my sources to ensure that I get good advice. My father did not believe in making accusations or pointing fingers at scapegoats. I think he found it a useless ploy to blame people for mistakes I should have been smart enough to avoid.

I remember a situation when I really irritated my father because I wanted to act before getting good advice. My father had agreed to help me buy my first new car. As you might imagine I was overly anxious. I took it upon myself to get the transaction started. I visited the local Chevrolet dealership to shop and compare models. I was completely unprepared and inexperienced.

The salesman appeared nice enough. He showed me around. The more interest I displayed, the pushier he became. Before leaving the dealership I signed a sales order I did not understand for a vehicle way over my budget. It seemed like a good idea at the time.

My father was angry. He asked why I went around him and started negotiating a transaction when I had absolutely no experience. He said, "You do not know what you are doing." Afterward, he stopped talking to me about buying a car. It felt like weeks before we would discuss the topic again. I thought he was punishing me. Later I would learn he was teaching me a lesson.

One day my father said, "It is time to buy a car." We went to the dealership and selected an appropriately priced model. Next we drove to the bank to speak to the loan officer. It was obvious from the outset that the loan officer was expecting us. The loan was preapproved. The deal was made beforehand. The whole transaction was smooth and fast.

Later, my father would explain. He said, "Son, you should get advice before making any big decisions in a matter where you don't have experience. People in a business transaction can be eager to take advantage of you." He explained further by noting that my previous attempt to purchase a car was premature. I had no negotiating experience. I did not know from whence the financing could come. I had not asked for advice from the right people.

As it turned out, the salesman from the earlier deal never pressed me to return and finalize the transaction. I suppose he recognized my inexperience as well. I did not return to cancel the sales contract.

I apologized for the aggravation I had created. He said, "Now you've learned a valuable lesson. Don't forget it."

—≪◆≫—

THE PRACTICAL APPLICATION

The idea of seeking help from competent sources seems obvious on its face. After all, who would intentionally ask for assistance from people who are ill equipped to be helpful? We are all subject to getting the wrong advice from time to time. These errors in judgment often lead to unfortunate results. The lessons I learned from my father are both practical and philosophical.

Let's start with a fundamental premise. Everyone needs help at some point in their lives. The world celebrates mavericks, self-made success stories, and solitary heroes. This fantasy makes for entertaining Hollywood lore, but the real world doesn't usually work this way. People are at their best when they collaborate with others to leverage their experiences and insights.

It is unadulterated hubris for an individual to conclude that he does not need the contributions of others to be at his best. Think about this notion for a moment: It is a false assumption to believe that one possesses all the unilateral knowledge, skills, and abilities needed to achieve success. Therefore, to be successful in life and business, one must accept one's own limitations and embrace the necessity of leveraging help.

Well, if it is so generally understood that we should only accept the help of people who are most qualified to help, why do we sometimes get the wrong advice? The answer may lie in our judgment of what makes good advice. Good advice has three important elements:

1. Good advice should come from someone who has a body of work that provides evidence of competence in the relevant area.
2. Good advice should be accompanied by empirical facts to support the suggestion.
3. The adviser should be prepared to defend his advice when challenged.

My father insisted that I should only consider following the advice of someone who knows what she is talking about. To his way of thinking, you should test competence by looking at a person's work experience. If my father sought counsel from a farmer, that farmer should have productive crops on the farm. If that farmer's crops were failing, my father would not be inclined to follow the advice. If someone lacks success in a field, advice from that person will likely be lacking in effect.

In the business world we hire consultants and vendors based on their client lists. If a vendor demonstrates positive work products with other clients similarly situated to our industry, then we have more confidence that the vendor can help us achieve our objectives. If a proposal shows no indication that the consultant has ever completed an assignment like the one that faces us, we are skeptical about any claims of competence in this area.

We remind ourselves that the reason for hiring a particular company, vendor, or consultant is that we lack the skill set on our own to complete the objective. We are seeking help in an area where we have a weakness. No company seeks to hire a consultant who knows less than the company officials. For this reason, references are verified and background checks are made to ensure that the help sought is competent.

The second element for good advice is empirical evidence. One of the reasons we fall for the wrong advice is not testing the assertions with proof. Advice that is given without the discipline of proof can be dangerous to follow, because relying on erroneous advice can lead to bad assumptions. Bad assumptions can then lead to ill-informed decisions. Ill-informed decisions can cause unintended results.

I have observed that people are quick to give advice on any number of subjects. We see this on cable news channels every day. The talkers make declarations without supporting facts. Perhaps the talkers are playing to a short-attention-span TV audience, or maybe it's just the lack of time, but commentators often do not offer facts to back up their assertions. The viewing audience is left to accept the edicts at face value. Without supporting facts, any decisions made to change business strategies are basically uninformed. It is incumbent upon those of us who receive advice to test the assumptions to make sure the advice is applicable for our purposes.

The third element for good advice is expressing a healthy level of skepticism. I find that the first round of advice may not offer the most thoughtful direction one can receive. When seeking advice, you should push back a little to see if the adviser has thoroughly considered all the options, probable and otherwise. If one's inclination is to default immediately to the first piece of advice given, little opportunity and appetite may exist to explore further. Without a degree of pushback, how might one know if better choices are available?

Advice is fallible if it fails to consider all the possibilities. Most decisions in life involve options beyond yes and no. The value of collaborating with others is that we discover new opportunities. This exploration often reveals to us the complexity of a situation beyond our initial impressions. If the exploration reveals new realities, then we have moved beyond the risk that hubris presents. We are now ready to engage with others for the best help toward achieving our optimal result.

THE VALUE OF A GOOD NAME

My last name is Smith. There is nothing spectacular about this surname. In fact, it's rather commonplace. Besides "Jones," "Smith" seems to be the moniker most often used to illustrate an everyday name.

I knew my name was ordinary as the world perceives it. However, in my household, I was taught that the Smith name was a badge of honor to be worn proudly. From my earliest memories my father emphasized the importance of a good name and my responsibility for keeping the Smith name in high regard.

My father often pulled a prank on people he would meet. It went like this.

He would ask unsuspecting folks if they knew that at one point everyone in the world was once named Smith. Puzzled, most folks were astonished at this revelation. He then would say that when someone did something wrong, they would be kicked out of the family and given a new name. "What is your last name?" he would ask again. "'Jackson'? So what did your family do to get the name 'Jackson'?"

I'm not sure if most people appreciated his brand of humor, but he sure enjoyed the punch line. I grew up hearing that story told with comic intent, but underlying the joke was my father's strong belief in the value of a good name. He would reinforce this notion to me throughout my childhood.

My father repeatedly told me that the family name I inherited meant something in the community. He said he had a responsibility to pass along to me a name that had a good reputation. The reason is that a good name would give me a head start in life. People would judge me by my name and family reputation long before I arrived. He emphasized that his gift to me of a good family name was a property to be cherished and protected as I moved into the world. My responsibility in return would be to deliver an equally good or better name to my offspring and generations beyond them.

My father would remind me of the accomplishments of Smiths in my lineage. The Smiths were entrepreneurs. My family owned businesses, attended colleges, served in community organizations, and participated in local politics. Smiths were advocates for people's rights. Smiths were land developers and property owners. My father said he mentioned these attributes only to establish within me the expectation that I would further advance the family name in productive ways. He said that whatever the Smiths had accomplished before, I would do even greater things. I wasn't completely sure what he meant by that prophecy, but I took his charge as a direction to be industrious in life.

Growing up in a small town, it seemed that there was added weight placed on a family's reputation. People would often generalize about members of a family based on the actions of a few. If the most notorious members of a family had a bad reputation, other members would be so labeled.

My father emphasized that one's associates mattered. He advised that if I took up with people who had bad habits, I would be subject to the same predilections. Rather than rising to my potential, the influence of the crowd would be a drag on my progress.

My father encouraged me to seek the companionship of people who would be a positive influence on me. He wasn't implying that I should shun others. On the contrary, he recommended that I *not* judge a person's integrity or reputation based on the family name. I should look at a person's body of work to gauge how productive that person has been. Such investigation was necessary so that I would associate with people who would be uplifting and inspiring to me.

THE PRACTICAL APPLICATION

As the saying goes, "Birds of a feather flock together." The idea is that people tend to associate with those who share their interests, personalities, tastes, and outlooks. I'm not sure if this applies for all family members, but our families obviously influence us.

While my father focused on the reputations and traits of families, his thinking can also be applied to professional networks, business associates, and company cultures. If a company is known for a certain manner of conduct, it stands to reason that the company's employees will share the same reputation. Therefore, one's occupation can have an impact on a person's reputation in the community.

We learn in marketing about affinity among members of a target group. A common bond exists among individuals in the same community, age group, income bracket, profession, religion, and ethnicity. This common bond helps marketers bundle services and improve their products' appeal to potential customers, which helps companies sell their wares to a certain market. One should ask how he can leverage his group's reputation to better position himself for success.

My father would first suggest that we make sure the family—in this case, the group—has a good reputation. Regardless of whether you are most identified as being part of a social, professional, or demographic group, think how much the group's reputation accurately reflects your values. If the group's reputation and your values are in alignment, you may want to leverage the group's good name for your benefit. If a misalignment is present between how you want to be seen and how your group is judged, you need to overcome those deficits.

One need not be captive to a family's reputation. Being part of a group that has a bad reputation need not cast a fatal and final light on any individual. People can rehabilitate their reputation and family name. Salvaging a negative name begins with one person and a series of single positive deeds.

The opposite of a good name is a bad name. Bad names are generally associated with negative character traits—deficiencies such as dishonesty, undisciplined ethics, and slothfulness. People who illustrate these characteristics are considered undependable, not trustworthy, and unreliable.

Repair of a family name begins with exhibiting positive traits. It is not enough to simply proclaim that one has positive traits. A good reputation is earned with action. This is slow work and may take years to manifest.

From time to time, some companies have to fix their

reputations. The negative light may have come about from a flawed product, wrongful conduct of its leaders, or an unethical approach to commerce. When this happens, company leaders often try to restore their reputation with a carefully crafted public relations campaign.

One can learn a great deal about restoring a name by observing the approaches organizations take to overcome a public scandal. The generally accepted wisdom is to admit the wrongdoing and pledge to do better. The organizations' leaders are usually apologetic and remorseful for the misdeeds. A public gesture is sometimes offered to make amends for these missteps, such as a company that publicizes a substantial donation to a cause or committing funds for a purpose.

Some organizations fail the test when it comes to rehabilitating their reputations. They act with impunity toward their stockholders, customers, regulators, and employees. This approach doesn't usually work for companies, individuals, or social groups. In some instances, the best course for recuperation is replacing the CEO and purging the ranks of senior management. This is a hard way to learn a lesson. The best advice for company leadership obviously is to avoid altogether scenarios that lead to reputational damage.

Company reputations are like family names. The public will praise or condemn both based on the perception of character and deeds. To secure the most positive name, choose associates and actions wisely. The benefits and consequences can have a long-lasting impact.

THE BURDEN OF LEADERSHIP

was relatively young when I achieved my first management position at the credit union. My title was vice president / city executive. Essentially, I was responsible for managing a branch office. The duties included overseeing the lending, teller, and member services functions. Suddenly, it seems, I had twenty people reporting to me and relying on my judgment to make the office run smoothly.

The job required long hours and hard work. I was the first to arrive in the morning and the last person to lock up nearly every day. I spent most weekends in the office working the collections list, writing reports, and reviewing office performance. I was young and had the drive to push through long days and weeks.

The risk of continuously working grueling hours is that one may get fatigued. I experienced that. The weekends were not long enough to recover from one week before the next week would begin. My sleep patterns were not consistent. Some days it was hard to concentrate. I felt like this approach to my work was not sustainable. I was afraid I was failing at being a leader.

I wondered if there was an easier way to manage my career. In fact, I considered whether management was for me at all. Perhaps I would be happier in a non-management role that required no overtime and in which my weekends would be all to myself.

One day I saw an advertisement for an office worker for a public company. The position seemed unchallenging. The salary was not particularly appealing. I thought it could be welcoming to go to a regular nine-to-five job, leave at the end of the day, and have my evenings and weekends to myself. I submitted a résumé and application for the job. Soon I was called for an interview.

I remember the day of the interview very well. The

interviewer was working in a small, cramped, utilitarian office. He asked me to take a seat. He proceeded to methodically read the interview questions one at a time. To this point he still had not made eye contact with me. He just went from one question to the next in a monotone.

I sat there looking at him. He did not seem happy with his job. In fact, his countenance was depressed and lifeless. I began to feel sorry for him. Glancing at the family pictures on his bookshelf and knickknacks on his desk, I imagined his life outside of this office. I wondered whether, if I accepted this job, this would happen to me.

I interrupted the interviewer before he could ask another question. I thanked him for his time and said I was withdrawing my name from consideration for the job. At this point, he looked up from his papers for the first time and showed an emotion. He asked why. I simply said the job was not for me. I politely excused myself and left.

I told my father about this experience. I admitted to my weariness with leadership positions. I confessed that sometimes I just wanted to be one of the fellas. My father listened.

My father's advice to me about life evolved over time. When I was a small boy he dictated what I should do. There was little conversation about his directives. I was simply to do what I was told. When I became a teen-ager, the advice became a conversation. My father would ask me what I thought about a situation or a task. He required me to stand and defend my answers. Now that I was an adult with adult responsibilities, my father's advice became reviews of lessons he already taught me. I just needed to be reminded of what I already knew.

My father heard my complaints about the burdens of management. It was hard work and was taking a toll on me. He listened patiently and told me that I had no choice in the matter. I was built for leadership. He stated that he prepared me from the time I was a small child to take the reins of my life. He said, "You were destined to be called upon to take a leadership role everyplace you go."

He advised that leadership follows some people no matter where they are. He recapped situations where I seemed to end up in a leadership role. Even when I sought to sit quietly and just be part of the crowd, someone would tap me on the shoulder and insist on greater involvement. In each instance I would think, *Why can't I just be left alone to be an observer?* My father insisted I would not be able to escape this calling in my life. This was my destiny.

My father reminded me that I found hanging out on the corner with the fellas to be unfulfilling. He said, "You thought you were missing something, only to find out later that your life is to mean something greater than idle wastes of time." He repeated the tales he shared with me in the cab of his truck on our long rides to the Columbia, South Carolina, farmers' market. He told me stories about what it means to be a man and to take on the responsibility of raising a family. My father said the reason he turned everything into a lesson is that I would need these stories to fall back on when I was an adult. When times grew difficult, I would have a wellspring of lessons and stories to relate to a situation.

My father explained why he pushed me all those years. He said, "I knew you needed to be a critical thinker, smart businessman, and hard worker. This was all for getting you ready to be a leader in life." He reminded me I was a leader in high school. He said, "You were reluctant then, but you grew into the role. And that was just the beginning. Leadership will always be a part of who you are. You cannot escape this demand on your life. You will be called to a management role everywhere you go. You just have to accept the burden of leadership."

This was not quite the sympathy I was seeking, but it was what I needed to hear.

THE PRACTICAL APPLICATION

For as long as I can remember, my father was always in a leadership role. He was a leader in our extended family. When family members needed help solving a problem, they would call my father. He could often be found dispensing advice on how to succeed at a task or endeavor.

I observed my father as a leader in the community in various capacities. He was a deacon in our hometown Baptist church, a thirty-second-degree Mason, chairman of the Sanitary District Board, a member of the historical society, and a Brunswick County commissioner. He participated in numerous other roles and positions.

Leadership comes with a cost. Leaders often endure personal and professional sacrifices. The challenges of serving the public or an organization can exact a toll. So, naturally, I wondered why my father persisted in serving in various leadership roles.

One must surmise that the benefits of leadership outrank the cost of being out front on an issue. To get a fair sense of the pros and cons of leadership, let's compare them.

The benefits of leadership include the development of oneself to exploit one's talents to their full potential. Quite often leaders must undertake a difficult task and pursue an obstacle-filled course of action. Leaders usually face resistance to their ideas and actions. I suppose if there were no opposition, a movement would not need leaders.

By assuming responsibility for an endeavor, a leader builds the tenacity, talents, and abilities to be successful in one's craft. Think of the resistance encountered when exercising with weights. The body's muscles get stronger by stretching against an opposing force. Challenges do the same for a leader's abilities.

The burden of leadership includes having on one's mind the weight of others' concerns. A good leader recognizes the stakeholders who rely on the leader's performance. When I look around my office at my fellow employees, I don't just see my colleagues alone. Each teammate has others in their lives who rely upon them for support in some way. It could be a spouse, significant other, children, parents, friends, and so on. Given this revelation, I apply a multiplier effect to the number of stakeholders who count on me to make good leadership judgments. These are all the folks whom my performance affects in one manner or another.

A good leader feels the weight of all those stakeholders who have an interest in his workmanship. The weight keeps the leader sober and serious about his responsibilities. Now, this weight must be considered with a sense of balance. Otherwise, one could become overwhelmed by the voices and needs of so many others. If not carefully well-adjusted, the leadership weight can become a burden too heavy to carry.

HIDDEN WORKS

I chose this example as the final essay in this collection because this life lesson would be one of the last acts I would share with my father. This story is special for so many reasons. The illustrations here are examples of his personality, values, and commitments to others.

My father taught me that everyone has an enduring responsibility to help others. He taught this lesson not so much by words but through his deeds. What's remarkable about his devotion to philanthropy was his insistence that his good acts be a secret. Moreover, he focused his charity on helping individuals who had few other resources.

My father received great satisfaction from assisting

others, but not just anyone. He was committed to helping elderly people who were poor. He provided assistance in several ways. His only request in return for these good deeds was that he remain anonymous.

Growing crops on a farm for sale in the market yields two grades of produce. Number One harvests were the vegetables that were in showman condition for the store shelves. The cucumbers must be long and straight. The choice tomatoes were selected for the absence of blemishes. The squash had to be without any scars and even in tone and color.

As with all crops, some yields were not in perfect condition. These items were called Number Two crops. There were visible marks, disfigurations, or discoloration on some of the items. Essentially, there was nothing wrong with the crops' taste or quality. They were just considered cosmetically unappealing to the public.

Some farmers discarded Number Two crops by letting the yields rot in the fields. In some instances, the rejected crops were fed to livestock. My father saw this as an opportunity to feed hungry people.

My father would gather the excess crops and hand

deliver them at no charge to elderly people, single mothers, and low-wealth neighbors. These charitable deliveries would often be made during the very early morning hours before most people were awake for the day. He would leave the produce on their front doorsteps to be discovered later that morning.

One morning while accompanying my father on an early morning delivery, I asked why he dropped off food so early in the mornings. He said he had too much to do to get caught up in lots of conversation. This way he could leave the gifts, not be delayed, and be on his way. I understood his argument for efficiency, but I think the real reason is that he did not want to be recognized for what he saw as his reasonable Christian service.

After retiring from operating the vegetable market, my father continued to grow crops in the fields. This time, he did not sell vegetables to the public. He gave away the entire yield to people who had the need. After supplying neighbors with the greatest need, he would invite able-bodied adults to harvest their own vegetables from his fields for free. He believed that if you were able to work, you should work to help yourself.

My father's deeds did not stop at free vegetable deliveries. Later we would discover more charitable works he performed in the community.

In 2004, members of the community wanted to surprise my father with their appreciation. The day was called "Bubba's Day." Dozens of people turned out to salute him. Individual after individual took turns at the microphone testifying to my father's kindness and generosity. I think he was embarrassed that all this testimony was coming out, but he was still gracious, of course.

I learned a lot at Bubba's Day. I heard tales of free vegetables, donated firewood, purchased heating oil, fixed roofs, free rents, vehicle repairs, and many other acts of assistance. We had no idea he was doing all this for our neighbors. He had not been altogether forthcoming with his own family.

Shortly before my father passed away, his health was visibly declining. He was no longer able to drive himself. He spent most of his days sitting in his recliner. One weekend I was keeping him company in the living room when he asked me to give him a ride.

We drove into Southport. He directed me down a

street and onto a dirt road. We turned right onto a path through the woods to an old mobile home. He told me he'd be back in a few minutes. He struggled to walk to the front door. After knocking, an elderly lady opened the door. He put something in her hands and, without saying anything to her, turned to walk back to the car. Once inside, he said, "Let's go."

I did not ask what it was all about, nor did he volunteer an explanation. The expression on that old lady's face told me all I needed to know.

THE PRACTICAL APPLICATION

Hidden works are about more than having sympathy and compassion for others. There is no doubt that performing charity is an endearing human behavior. Showing kindness to others is an admirable trait. The hidden lesson here is the value we all receive in return for helping our neighbors.

My father was convinced that we are stronger as a community than we are as individuals. The notion of being a self-made person is largely a fiction. We need

each other to realize success for our community and ourselves. Shared charity is just one of the ways the public
redistributes resources for the benefit of the whole. The
other way is through the normal course of commerce.

Most people associate the exchange of goods and services through merchandising channels as the way society redistributes resources. When one purchases a good
or service from a retail establishment, an exchange of
resources takes place. In most instances, the exchange
involves money for goods or services. Through this
transaction, a surplus good is exchanged to meet a def-
icit need. This occurred on the farm with the sale of
Number One–graded vegetables.

The other way communities redistribute resources
is through charitable works. Members of society take
surplus resources and channel them to people who have
needs. My father did this with his early-morning deliveries and other acts. Unlike a commercial transaction
where there is an exchange of money for goods, a charitable act appears to be unilateral. In other words, the
donor gets nothing for his deeds, but that's not the case.

I wondered, other than being a nice person, what

would possess my father to work so hard in the fields of his farm to give away his produce? Further, why would he covertly help people in the community without any expectation of compensation? I figured there must be more to this than what appeared on the surface. I believe the answer is in the benefit of communal good.

In the study of economics, there is the notion of scarcity. Essentially, there are the haves and the have-nots. If we think of economics in purely selfish terms, for there to be winners, there must be some losers. If that's so, then to be successful, we should count on some people being failures. This outlook begs the question: is it possible to have all winners in a community and root out all failures?

If my father had gone about his charitable deeds and publicized what he did to the whole community, he still would have been celebrated. The problem is that the community would recognize him as a success and the people he helped as failures. The economic principle of scarcity would come into play. But if he could quietly help less fortunate neighbors become successful, he would gain by being part of a community where more people apparently have sufficient resources. He would have reduced the perceived scarcity and improved upon the opportunities for success.

This lesson teaches me that we should be uncomfortable with our own successes if we have neighbors who experience scarcity. I have come to accept that nothing is wrong with being successful. However, my father taught that our success is incomplete if we are not helping others. My father demonstrated this value with his life. We would all do well to emulate his example with our actions.

Because of the teachings of my father and observations over a nearly four-decade-long career, I am consumed with the notion of economic development and empowerment. I have witnessed firsthand the disparities that exist between communities. I believe the availability of financial services, employment opportunities, affordable foods, healthcare, and education travels largely along economic tracks.

I wanted to know why. Most communities have two sides of the clichéd railroad tracks. On one side live the wealthy or solidly middle-class citizens. There are clues that identify these neighborhoods as such: the sizes of the homes, the number of bays in the garages, the manicured lawns and conditions of the homes, the proximity to shopping and services, the quality of vehicles in the driveway. These signs signal an affluent community.

On the other side of the tracks we discover a different scenario. These citizens have less economic means. There are clues that identify these neighborhoods, too: the sizes of the homes, the number of bays in the garages or the lack of garages altogether, the conditions of the lawns and homes, the distance from shopping and services, the quality of vehicles in the yard. These signs signal a community that is less than wealthy.

When I ask my friends who work in different occupations to contrast the communities, I get stark comparisons. My friend who is a social worker says the frequency of family triage cases seems to be higher on the low-wealth side of town. My colleague who is a police officer says the number of reported crimes is higher with lower economic conditions. My associates who are firefighters report on the fire and health hazards in homes in poorer neighborhoods.

I don't mean to imply that wealthy communities don't have social ills. They do. The challenge with less wealthy communities and families is that they have significantly less resources to rebound from social challenges.

I believe my calling into the world of finance took

place for a reason. My destiny was to seek opportunities to help individuals improve their economic plight. I have this Pollyannaish faith that someday I will uncover a secret formula to economic prosperity. I hope to find a way to lift people out of poverty. I want to discover the means to solve social problems through financial empowerment.

If I were to seek advice from my father today on this calling, I believe he would point me back to the lessons he taught me over the years. I believe I have all the tools I need to succeed. I just not have found the right formula or set of circumstances to fulfill this mandate on my life ... yet.

Made in the USA
Columbia, SC
18 April 2019